THE NEW ASTRONOMY

PROBING THE SECRETS OF SPACE

FRED D'IGNAZIO

A GROLIER COMPANY

FRANKLIN WATTS
NEW YORK/LONDON/TORONTO/SYDNEY/1982
A FIRST BOOK

FRONTIS: THE WHIRLPOOL GALAXY,
IN CANES VENATICI M-51

Cover photograph of the Hale Observatories and
Telescope courtesy of Hale Observatories (Copyright © 1959 by California Institute of Technology and Carnegie Institution of Washington.)

Interior photographs courtesy of Holiday Film
Corp.: pp. 6 and 53; Lick Observatory: pp. 11
and 22; United Press International: p. 18; the
New York Public Library Picture Collection: p.
32; Mt. Hopkins Observatory: p. 38; The National
Radio Astronomy Observatory: p. 42; NASA: pp.
47 and 49 (both); Hale Observatories (Copyright
© 1959 by California Institute of Technology and
Carnegie Institution of Washington.): p. 59.

Library of Congress Cataloging in Publication Data

D'Ignazio, Fred.
The new astronomy.

(A First book)
Bibliography: p.
Includes index.
Summary: Explains how astronomers are using
new kinds of telescopes, computerized cameras,
and space probes to generate new theories about the
universe and its mysteries.
1. Astronomy—Juvenile literature.   2. Cosmology
—Juvenile literature.   [1. Astronomy.   2. Universe.
3. Space sciences]   I. Title.
QB46.D53   520   81-21817
ISBN 0-531-04386-X   AACR2

CONTENTS

FOR MIKE LETTS, BILL LETTS,
AND MAHLON EASTERLING

CHAPTER ONE

WHAT IS THE NEW ASTRONOMY?

Four-and-a-half centuries ago, people believed that the sun, stars, and planets circled the earth on whirling spheres. Then, in the early 1500s, the Polish astronomer Nicolaus Copernicus shocked the world by declaring that the earth spun like a top and, along with the other planets, circled the sun. Copernicus wrote a book about his new ideas. His book was the blueprint for a "new astronomy."

Today, in the 1980s, we are entering a period in astronomy that may be as revolutionary as the age of Copernicus. Today, an army of astronomers from all around the world are using incredible space-age tools to create a flood of new ideas and raise many new questions about the universe. This new astronomy is again making the universe seem strange and different.

Astronomers are often separated from what they study by millions of years, trillions of miles, and a clouded window of air called the atmosphere. To overcome these obstacles, today's astronomers are building huge telescopes in the clean air of deserts, on mountaintops, and on the rims of volcanoes. They are using computerized cameras and superfast film to capture faint and blurry starlight. They are working with other scientists who are constructing atom-smashers the size of small towns to blast matter apart and discover what it is made of.

An even better way to see the universe is from above the atmosphere. Astronomers have put telescopes aboard high-flying airplanes, balloons, orbiting satellites, and space stations. They have built robot space probes, equipped them with telescopes, and shot them toward the sun, moon, and planets. They will soon send up the giant Space Telescope that will enable us to see farther into space than ever before.

Today's astronomers are also using new kinds of telescopes to detect and record radiation that is invisible to the human eye. Astronomers are mapping the universe's remote sections with help from radio, infrared, ultraviolet, gamma-ray, and X-ray telescopes. Even more unusual telescopes are on the way.

To better understand what they see, astronomers are teaming up with other space scientists, including planetologists and geophysicists. Together they are generating new ideas about how the universe was born, how it has grown up, and how it may die. They are chasing down the microscopic building blocks of the universe, such as the neutrino, the quark, and antimatter. And they are searching for explanations for the strange things they see, such as pulsating energy beacons, galaxy-gobbling black holes, and gigantic gas jets that appear to travel at 40 times the speed of light.

Compared to the vastness of the universe, the earth is a mere flyspeck whirling through space. Yet it is our home.

By learning more about the universe, we may solve some mysteries here on earth. And by learning more about the earth, we probe deeper into the secrets of space.

CHAPTER TWO

A UNIVERSE OF STORMS

You may not think of the earth as a particularly violent or stormy place. But it can be.

The earth spawns tornadoes that rip towns apart. Earthquakes topple cities, and volcanoes blow the tops off mountains. Hurricane winds suck up the ocean and drop it in barrels on the land, sometimes drowning entire seacoasts.

Yet the earth's violence is like a flickering candle compared to the blazing violence in most other parts of the universe. There, supergiant stars explode and incinerate whole star systems and even large sections of galaxies. Incredibly dense neutron stars rock with starquakes that blast dangerous radiation across billions of miles of space. Black holes may collide then rebound across galaxies like spikes jabbing through an inner tube. Flying asteroid "mountains" smash into planets and their moons with the force of 100 billion tons of dynamite. It is thought that the universe itself began with an enormous bang, in an oven so hot it would have vaporized a million suns.

Today, astronomers are often witness to the sudden, violent changes that end the lives of stars and galaxies and give birth to new ones. But this was not always so.

Look into the nighttime sky. You will see hundreds, maybe thousands, of twinkling stars nestled in soft, velvety blackness. Maybe you will also see the glistening trail of a meteor or the silver cradle of the moon. What you will see is a universe at peace. You will hear no deafening roars, no mind-numbing explosions. Gliding peacefully across the sky, the stars and moon never make a sound. The sky appears silent and at rest.

Except for an occasional comet or meteor, this is the sky humans have seen for thousands of years. No wonder early astronomers pictured the universe as a tranquil and unchanging place. Compared to the violence and change they saw regularly on the earth, the universe seemed peaceful and changeless.

Occasionally the violence of the universe intruded. In A.D. 1054, Chinese astronomers noticed a bright splash of light in the constellation of Taurus (the Bull). Almost nine hundred years later an American astronomer, Edwin Hubble, looked through a powerful telescope and saw the gigantic Crab Nebula—an immense cloud of dust and gas—splattered across billions of miles. Hubble concluded that the nebula might have been formed from the *supernova,* or star explosion, seen by the Chinese in 1054.

In 1604, Johannes Kepler, Galileo Galilei, and other astronomers saw the last supernova to occur to date in our own galaxy. But as astronomers have invented bigger telescopes that see farther into space, they have discovered a vast number of new galaxies. By observing these, astronomers have witnessed hundreds of stars exploding, popping like firecrackers in the nighttime sky.

The Crab Nebula

—10

At the time of Copernicus people thought that the universe was perfect as well as peaceful. Then Galileo pointed his telescope at the moon and found it was pockmarked with craters. He studied the sun and found it had sunspots—giant black blemishes that moved across its surface.

People also believed for many centuries that the sun and planets revolved around the earth, though astronomers such as Copernicus and Galileo argued otherwise. Only slowly was a sun-centered solar system accepted. Then, in the late 1700s, the English astronomer William Herschel discovered that the sun was only one of more than a billion stars, all traveling through space together in a vast "island universe." He named this giant star island, or galaxy, the Milky Way.

Using his telescope, Herschel also saw objects in the sky that looked like fuzzy patches. He wondered if those patches might be other island universes. A hundred and fifty years later the American astronomer Edwin Hubble discovered that Herschel's fuzzy patches were indeed other galaxies. The Milky Way was just one of many galaxies adrift in the vast ocean of space. And our solar system was not even near the center of its own galaxy, but midway out on one of its rotating, spiral arms.

THE EXPLODING UNIVERSE

In 1924, Hubble was looking through the powerful telescope at the Mount Palomar Observatory in California and taking pictures of distant galaxies using an instrument called a *spectrograph.* The photographs of starlight taken using this instrument are called *spectrograms.*

Spectrograms are bands of color, from deep violet to crimson red. They are produced by separating the many different colored wavelengths of light contained in a star's normal "white" light. Spectrograms reveal what elements a star is made of, in which direction the star is heading, and how fast it is moving.

When Hubble looked at spectrograms from distant galax-

—12

ies, he was puzzled. They were surprisingly different from those of stars in our own galaxy.

Hubble was aware of an effect discovered in the 1840s by an Austrian physicist named Christian Doppler. The so-called *Doppler effect* then referred only to an increase or decrease in the frequency of sound waves caused by an object's motion.

You can hear this effect by listening to a train whistle or a siren on a fire truck or police car. Let's say you are at a train station. When a train approaches you at high speed, you hear its whistle as a high-pitched, almost shrill sound, like the high note of a piccolo or flute. Then, after the train whizzes past, its whistle sounds more like a low note on a tuba.

What is happening is that the approaching train's sound waves are increasing in frequency because of the train's movement toward you. You hear these "bunched-up" waves as a high-pitched sound. After the train has passed, its movement away from you causes a decrease in frequency of the sound waves. You hear these "stretched-out" waves as a low-pitched sound.

Light waves can also be altered by the Doppler effect. The movement of a star or galaxy toward the earth causes its light waves to increase in frequency and become a deeper blue or violet. The movement of a star or galaxy away from the earth causes its light waves to decrease in frequency and become longer and more reddish. This altering of light waves to the red or blue end of the spectrum is called a *shift.*

Hubble realized he was seeing a Doppler effect with light waves instead of sound waves. As he pointed his telescope at one distant galaxy after another, he saw starlight that showed enormous shifts toward the red, or long-wave, end of the spectrum. This meant that all the galaxies were receding from the earth.

In 1927, Hubble met with Vesto Slipher, an astronomer with the Lowell Observatory in Flagstaff, Arizona. Slipher had spent several years studying distant nebulae and had found that, based on their red shift, they seemed to be receding from the earth at speeds of up to 1,000 miles (1,600 km) a second.

Using Slipher's observations along with his own, Hubble discovered a definite relationship between a galaxy's red shift, its speed, and its distance from the earth. The farther away the galaxy was from the earth, the greater its red shift, and the faster it was moving.

Everywhere Hubble looked, galaxies were blasting away from the earth at enormous speeds. The universe showed little resemblance to the old picture of it as a peaceful, orderly place. To Hubble, it looked more like the aftermath of a gigantic explosion.

THE BIG BANG

One astronomer who learned of Hubble's observations tried to picture the universe in terms of a movie. If he froze the movie in the present and began playing it backward, he thought he might be able to trace the universe back to its origin.

The astronomer was Georges Lemaître, and in 1927 he played the "movie" back to its start. Lemaître calculated that somewhere between 12 and 20 billion years ago, all the matter in the universe was squeezed together inside a primeval "egg" or "atom." This densely packed egg became incredibly hot, and eventually it exploded, spewing energy and matter in all directions. This explosion became known as the *Big Bang.*

If the egg had been perfectly shaped, when it exploded it might have created a formless cloud of gas. Life might never have evolved. Fortunately, the egg contained "lumps" and "knots." When it exploded it threw its contents out in huge clods. These were the "seeds" for planets, stars, and galaxies.

Over billions of years, stars and galaxies by the millions were born. These eventually died and were followed by new stars and new galaxies. The universe gradually cooled and continued to expand. At its edges, it was hurtling through space at enormous speeds.

—14

The Big Bang theory was supported by Hubble's and Slipher's observations, but to many astronomers there was still not enough evidence to prove that the Big Bang had been responsible for the creation of the entire universe. By the 1950s, a worldwide controversy had grown up concerning the origin of the universe. Astronomers on one side argued that all matter hadn't been created in a single explosion. It was being created continually throughout space. To those who argued for this "steady-state universe," the cosmos was infinite and eternal—without beginning or end. Astronomers on the other side of the debate argued for the Big Bang—for a finite universe created billions of years ago out of a single explosion.

Was the universe in a "steady state" or had it been created by the Big Bang? The answer did not come until the mid-1960s.

At the Bell Telephone Laboratories in Holmdel, New Jersey, Arno Penzias and Robert Wilson had spent most of the early 1960s working on an advanced type of microwave receiver. This receiver looked something like a huge alpine horn. It acted like a giant "ear" to listen for microwaves—short radio waves—carrying messages from communications satellites orbiting the earth.

In 1965, Penzias and Wilson finally completed construction of their receiver and switched it on. It appeared broken. Instead of the clear, clean sounds they expected to hear, they heard static—a faint hissing noise that sounded like an unlit burner on a gas stove.

The two astronomers spent the next few weeks trying to locate the source of the problem. First, they cleared a couple of nesting pigeons out of the inside of the receiver. Then they scrubbed the receiver thoroughly. When that didn't eliminate the noise, they took the antenna and receiver apart and completely rebuilt them. But the hiss wasn't gone. Now it was even louder than before.

In desperation, the two men contacted P. J. E. Peebles at

Princeton University and told him about the receiver's problem.

Peebles was one of the American astronomers trying to prove the theory of the Big Bang. He was fascinated to hear about the problems with the Bell Laboratories receiver. Perhaps the receiver wasn't broken at all, he said. Perhaps it was so good that it could "hear" something missed by earlier, less sensitive devices—namely, the faint background rush of radio waves. And maybe these waves were the "fallout" left over from the Big Bang.

It took Penzias, Wilson, and other scientists only a few months to build new, even more sensitive radio receivers and telescopes. These new devices confirmed the existence of the background radio waves. The waves, in turn, solidly supported the theory of the Big Bang. And if the universe had been created by the Big Bang, it couldn't be infinitely large, and it might not be eternal.

BLACK HOLES

Since the entire universe was now assumed to be the result of an explosion, it was easier to see how its parts, too, might be violent and explosive. Theories involving violence and change in the universe became more believable with the general acceptance of the Big Bang theory.

Almost two hundred years ago the French astronomer, Pierre Laplace, speculated about mysterious objects so strange that they caused the laws of physics to break down. Modern, twentieth-century astronomers continued Laplace's work and speculated about how massive stars might burn themselves out, blast off their outer "shells," then succumb to their own enormous gravity and collapse in upon themselves. The astronomers theorized that the result would be a *black hole*—an object with such overpowering gravity that light itself would be held captive. In fact, the object was even worse than a hole. After it dug the hole, it jumped in and pulled everything nearby in along with it.

Early in the twentieth century, the great German-born physicist Albert Einstein proposed a theory of the universe based on a new understanding of *gravitation* (or *gravity*), the "pull" exerted by all matter in the universe. Part of Einstein's theory stated that an enormously large and dense object, which has a very strong gravitational pull, could have a strange effect on time and space. The object's huge gravity could stretch out time and curve space in on itself.

Using Einstein's theories, scientists interested in black holes speculated that the pull of a black hole would be so great that even light could not escape it. But if a black hole "swallowed" light, how could it be seen through telescopes? How could astronomers check to see if black holes really existed?

This problem was handled in three ways. First, earth-based astronomers, using optical telescopes (telescopes that detect visible light), searched for stars and galaxies where strange things were happening. Something weird going on might mean a black hole was in the vicinity.

Second, by the middle of the twentieth century, new "windows" on the universe were being created in the form of telescopes that detected invisible forms of radiation such as X rays and gamma rays.

And finally, by the late 1960s and early 1970s, telescopes were being put aboard rocket ships and launched into space, beyond the earth's obscuring atmosphere. These telescopes were built to detect several kinds of radiation coming from space, including visible light, gamma rays, X rays, and ultraviolet rays. By the early 1970s, all of these "eyes" were looking for black holes.

Then, in December 1972, the X-ray satellite *Uhuru,* orbiting the earth, detected an object in the constellation of Cygnus (the Swan) that was emitting huge quantities of X rays. The source of the X rays was named Cygnus X-1 and was very possibly caused by matter spiraling into a black hole.

When optical astronomers searched the region of space

surrounding Cygnus X-1, they found a large, hot, blue super-giant star. Astronomers now speculate that Cygnus X-1 and the star are circling around each other and that Cygnus X-1 is gradually devouring the hot, blue star.

As Cygnus X-1 vacuums up the star and its matter, it heats up the atoms in the star's atmosphere to such great temperatures that the gas ionizes (sheds electrons) and eventually begins emitting X rays. These were the X rays detected by *Uhuru.*

Using telescopes and mathematical calculations, astronomers were able to determine that the diameter of Cygnus X-1 is only one quarter that of the earth. Yet despite its relatively small size, it contains more matter than ten suns smashed together. And, as it gobbles up more of its companion star, its gravity keeps growing.

Albert Einstein,
1879–1955

CHAPTER THREE

THE INVISIBLE UNIVERSE

All of us on earth are creatures of the earth. Our senses have evolved so that they are best suited for life on this planet. We can see only a narrow band of visible light (from red light to violet); we can hear only sounds of certain frequencies; and we feel comfortable only when the temperature of the air is neither too hot nor too cold.

Our picture of life and reality comes largely from our senses and from our experiences on the earth. But the earth is not typical of conditions elsewhere in the universe. In fact, it may be so unusual, and our sensory "windows" may be so narrow, that we are blind to much of the universe as it really is.

On the earth, almost everything is at a "happy medium"— just right for humans and other living things to survive and flourish. But the universe as a whole is different. It consists of enormous extremes. Our comfortable and (relatively) calm planet may be a rare island in a turbulent sea.

Take temperatures. On earth, the temperature rarely varies more than a few dozen degrees. In most of the universe, however, the temperature is a frigid, life-sapping cold of only a few degrees above absolute zero. (Absolute zero, −273° Centigrade or −459° Fahrenheit, is the theoretical point at which all molecular motion stops.) And in other places, such as in supernovae, there are firestorms millions of times hotter than the blazing core of the sun.

On earth, light enables us to sense the color, shape, and distance of everything around us. Light travels the short distances on earth almost instantly. Yet when we look at the universe, the picture we get from light alone is about as clear as trying to watch a scratchy film of an old baseball game taken from the outfield bleachers.

As fast as light travels, it takes the light from Andromeda, one of the "local" galaxies, over 2 million years to reach us. Even looking at a neighbor like Andromeda, we aren't looking at the present. We are looking at the distant past. In fact, we have no idea whether Andromeda even exists today. We are looking back in time to an Andromeda that existed over 2 million years ago, a time when humans still lived in caves.

Light is also a bad yardstick for calculating the size and shape of the universe. Light reaching us from distant galaxies can become greatly distorted when passing near the huge gravitational pull of objects such as neutron stars or black holes.

When we study the universe, time, too, takes on different dimensions. We are creatures who are born, live, and die all in a few decades. We measure time in seconds, hours, days, and years. But when we look at the universe, these units of time are not very meaningful. In the universe, most things happen either very quickly or very slowly. It takes millions of years for a planet to form. And a star like our sun may shine for billions of years. At the other extreme, the universe's building blocks—the particles inside the atom, for example—may be born, live, and die in less than a trillion trillionth of a second.

Finally, there is energy. The source of most of the earth's

energy is the sun. We see its energy in the form of visible light. We feel its energy as heat. Yet the sun is just a middling star, and many objects in the universe, such as black holes and neutron stars, can release more energy in a single second than the sun can in its whole lifetime.

The sun's *radiation*—all the forms of energy the sun emits—travels through space as particles called *photons.* Photons move in waves. The more energy the photon contains, the shorter the length of the wave and the greater the number of waves occurring.

Light waves contain many different wavelengths, some of which we perceive as visible light—all the colors of the rainbow. Each wavelength is composed of photons carrying a certain amount of energy. Most photons contain either more energy or less energy than photons that take the form of visible light. In other words, they travel in waves whose lengths are longer or shorter than those of visible light. High-energy photons, for example, have very short wavelengths. Depending on their length, these photons are called *gamma rays, X rays,* or *ultraviolet light.* Low-energy photons have much longer wavelengths. These photons are called *infrared radiation, microwaves,* or *radio waves.*

High-energy photons and low-energy photons account for most of a star's (or other energy source's) radiation. Yet to us, with our narrow, "tunnel" vision, this radiation is invisible.

In the last few years, astronomers and other scientists have invented instruments to detect the many forms of invisible radiation. These new instruments have greatly enlarged our view of the universe. They have helped to create the new astronomy.

The Andromeda Galaxy

CHAPTER FOUR

THE STRANGE SHAPE OF TIME AND SPACE

Try to imagine that in your hand you have a huge wad of wet bubble gum. You grab either end of the gum and stretch it out as far as you can without breaking it. Then you smash the gum back together into a small lump.

You have just conducted a "thought experiment"—an experiment you can perform using your imagination only. In this experiment, the wad of bubble gum represented the behavior of time and space in the presence of an object with enormous gravity.

But what if the gravity came from a black hole, an object whose gravity is so strong nothing can escape it? It is possible that a black hole's gravity could stretch time into eternity and squeeze space into nonexistence.

In your imagination pull on the gum again, so fast that it snaps, or squeeze it so hard that when you finish there's nothing left. This is what might happen to time and space in the vicinity of a black hole. The black hole's immense gravity might create a *singularity,* a central point where space and time are infinitely distorted, perhaps even causing a kind of "rip" in the universe.

Let's conduct another thought experiment. Imagine picking up a cannonball and heaving it onto a trampoline. After the cannonball stops bouncing, the trampoline will resemble the shape of time and space in the neighborhood of a massive object like the sun. In other words, they sag.

Now imagine that you have a marble, and you shoot it across the trampoline toward the cannonball. If you get the angle just right, the marble will loop in toward the cannonball, circle it, and whip back out and return to you.

You have just constructed a small model of a comet circling the sun. As far as the comet knows, it is traveling in a straight line. But in fact, the sun has bent space and time so much that the comet is actually traveling in an elliptical (egg-shaped) orbit.

Now imagine you have a powerful trash compactor that can squash anything. You run the cannonball through the compactor. It still has the same mass (amount of matter), so it comes out just as heavy. But now it has been squeezed to the size of a pea.

You run several more cannonballs through the compactor, then you squash all of the tiny cannonballs together into a superdense object the size of a golfball.

You put this "golfball" back on the trampoline, and you notice a new effect. The trampoline sags right to the ground, yet the width of the sag (its diameter) is much smaller.

What you have imagined now is a model of a *neutron star,* a star that has burst off its shell in a catastrophic explosion, then contracted into an enormously dense clump of neutrons. Neutrons are the tiny particles inside the nucleus, or center, of an atom.

Look at the sag. It is deep, and its sides are almost straight up and down. Doesn't it resemble a well? Your golfball and your trampoline are imitating the "gravity well" that is thought to exist in space and time around a neutron star. Anything that approaches the neutron star will be immediately affected by the sloping space near it; anything that gets too close will fall into the star's well.

For yet another thought experiment, imagine that, using your compactor, you were able to compress 10,000 cannonballs into an incredibly dense object the size and shape of a hockey puck. Your "puck" would weigh more than a million pounds (450,000 kg).

Using a fleet of heavy-duty cranes, you have the puck picked up and dropped into the center of the trampoline. What would happen? The puck wouldn't make the trampoline sag. It would puncture a hole right through it!

You have just imagined a simplified model of a black hole —an object so massive (yet so small) that it might pop a hole right through space and time. In the model, the trampoline represented our universe. When the puck ripped through the trampoline, it left our universe. Similarly, matter falling through a black hole might leave our universe.

Where might it go? Pretend that at the moment the puck was dropped you were on your hands and knees looking up at the underside of the trampoline. From that point of view, you would have seen the puck bursting through the canvas.

The trampoline's underside represents a "mirror universe." Some scientists have theorized that at the instant a black hole punctures a hole in our universe and disappears, it punctures a hole into a different universe and reappears— seemingly out of nowhere.

Now imagine that you turn the trampoline on its side and pinch the center of the canvas with pliers. You stretch the canvas out sideways as far as it will go without ripping. What have you created? Perhaps a model of our universe's true shape.

If our universe was indeed created by the Big Bang, it may not have formed into a perfect sphere. It may instead have folded up and stretched back in on itself. Enormous superclusters of galaxies; gigantic, invisible black holes; dark, cold nebulae; and dead, burnt-out stars might today be further warping the shape of space with their gravity. Our universe right now might look like a pretzel, a doughnut, or even a saddle.

Now suppose that instead of sucking matter and energy in, as black holes are thought to do, there were objects in the universe that spit out gigantic quantities of matter and energy. Have astronomers discovered any objects that appear to do this?

Yes. They are called the *quasars.*

Quasars were first discovered by the astronomer Maarten Schmidt in June 1963 at Mount Palomar Observatory in California. The name *quasar* comes from "quasi-stellar," or "star-like," object. Quasars seem to be the oldest and most distant objects in the universe. Since they are visible from so far away, they must be the brightest, most powerful objects in the universe, too. For example, one quasar, about the size of our solar system, is emitting more energy than a trillion suns. That's more energy than an entire galaxy!

Astronomers can only speculate on what kind of "fuel" the quasars are burning in order to generate such fantastic amounts of energy. Yet some think that quasars may be the flip side of black holes. Matter and energy may be disappearing from one part of our universe through a black hole, then reappearing in another part as a quasar. There may be no "mirror universe" at all.

CHAPTER FIVE

THE UNIVERSE INSIDE THE ATOM

There is an important branch of the new astronomy known as astrophysics. Astrophysicists study the effects that particles of matter even smaller than atoms have on the larger worlds of planets, stars, and galaxies. We are all made of stardust—matter blasted out of stars in their fiery death throes. And stardust is made of these tiny particles.

Most astronomers today believe that billions of years ago the universe was a single, unimaginably hot "egg." The egg exploded. Like a box of Roman candles thrown on a campfire, the egg fired great quantities of matter—in the form of high-energy particles—in every direction.

Over millions of years the universe cooled. As it cooled, the high-energy particles came together and formed the first atoms. Atoms clumped together and formed molecules. The molecules formed gases, and the gases gradually formed stars. One after another, the huge nuclear furnaces that power stars were ignited. Yet in spite of the heat given off by the stars, the universe as a whole continued to cool.

Today, the universe is a very cold place. Even the hottest stars are trillions of times cooler than the superheated cosmic egg was at the time of the universe's birth. Most of the tiny, high-energy particles that formed the early universe no longer exist by themselves. But there are exceptions. During frequent but brief periods of violence, and in certain corners of the universe, these particles suddenly reappear. By studying these sections of the universe, astronomers hope to find clues as to how the universe began.

Scientists have built devices known as particle accelerators. These huge machines boost the energy and speed of more familiar particles such as electrons and protons, then send them colliding and smashing into each other or into selected targets.

High-speed collisions turn the old particles into new ones such as neutrinos, quarks, and antimatter. Some of the new particles have incredibly short lifetimes; yet their tracks and trails can be recorded by computers and studied by scientists.

THE DEATH OF A PROTON

One place on earth where astrophysicists look for the elementary particles of matter is in an Ohio salt mine, nearly 2,000 feet (600 m) underneath the ground. There, and in several other locations around the world, scientists are building huge tanks filled with pure, distilled water. The tanks are monitored by computers and fitted with special devices that trap and amplify light.

Millions of neutrinos (see later in this chapter) and cosmic rays, which are given off by stars, stream into our atmosphere daily. When scientists conduct atom-smashing experiments on the surface of the earth, they are looking for unusual, short-lived particles. But sometimes it is hard to distinguish these from all the neutrinos and cosmic rays bouncing and whizzing about.

Deep underground, the number of cosmic rays is reduced

to almost zero, and the neutrinos by themselves don't present a problem. Scientists hope that in their huge underground tanks, out of all the trillions and trillions of protons contained inside the molecules of water, a single proton will do something they have never actually seen it do—die. And the scientists hope to capture the moment of its death with a supersensitive computerized camera.

To better understand what the scientists hope to see, let's journey down to the extremely small world of the proton—and beyond. Doing this will require several steps. It is something like opening boxes within boxes. Each time we open a box, we discover another box inside that is even smaller. Here, instead of boxes, we are opening particles (such as the atom), and finding other particles inside.

We start our journey with the molecules of water that fill the scientists' underground tanks. These molecules are incredibly small. It would take trillions of them to make enough water to fill an eyedropper. Yet the tanks are filled with thousands of tons of water.

If we look inside a water molecule, we find two hydrogen atoms and one oxygen atom. As small as molecules are, atoms are even smaller. Yet atoms are mostly empty space. When we look inside one, we find three kinds of particles—neutrons, protons, and electrons. In the center of the atom is a small nucleus, or core, of protons and neutrons. At the edges of the atom are its much smaller, orbiting electrons.

Protons are unbelievably small, yet they, too, are made up of still smaller particles called *quarks.* Quarks are elementary particles. This means that scientists believe that there are no other particles inside quarks. Quarks are so small that if a proton were the size of the solar system, a quark would be the size of a pea.

We can see now why it is so difficult for a proton to decay, or die. For this to happen, two quarks within the proton must bump into each other. But this is a very unlikely event, since the quarks inside a proton are relatively far apart. It is so unlikely that only a relatively small fraction of protons have died since the beginning of the universe.

But when quarks do collide, a particle called a *leptoquark* is created. The leptoquark survives only an instant. Then it decays into two other particles—a *positron* (an electron with a positive electrical charge) and an *antiquark* (a quark with an opposite charge). Should an antiquark meet a quark, the two will instantly explode. This will cause the proton to decay and emit gamma rays as a byproduct.

PULSARS AND
QUARK STARS

One way to observe quarks bumping into each other on the earth is to build those huge underground tanks just mentioned. But in other, hotter areas of the universe, quarks may still be crashing into each other on a grand scale.

In June 1967, radio astronomers in England sighted an object that acted like a lighthouse on a dangerous seacoast. Thirty times a second, the object sent a blast of radio waves across the universe. Astronomers called the object a *pulsar* and theorized that it may have been formed from a binary- (two-) star system consisting of a small neutron star and a companion star circling rapidly around it. Every time the neutron star emerged from behind the bigger, cooler star, it gave off radio waves that happened to be directed at the earth.

Over the years, dozens of pulsars have been detected. Yet astronomers are no longer sure that pulsars are actually neutron stars. Instead, some think they might be "quark stars," throwbacks to an earlier era of the universe when quarks existed freely in the universe.

Quark stars (if they exist), neutron stars, and black holes are all formed from huge, supergiant stars many times larger than our sun. Near the end of its life, a supergiant star uses up all of the hydrogen in its nuclear furnace, then blows off its

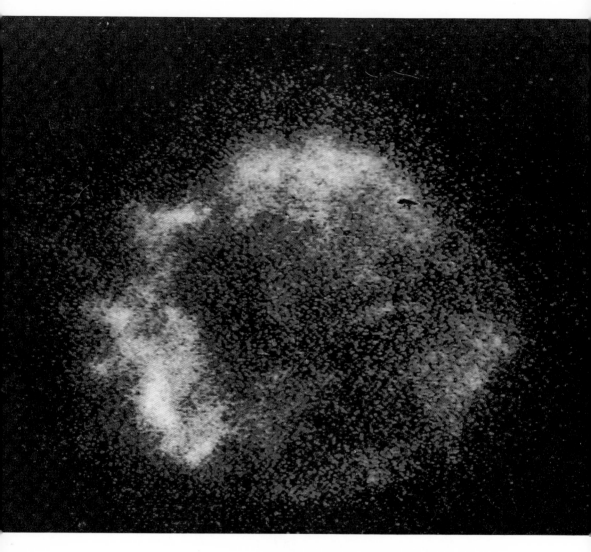

*This expanding shell of hot gas and debris
is all that is left of a massive star
that blew up in a supernova explosion.
The brightest areas represent X-ray emissions
given off as a result of the explosion.*

shell in a supernova explosion that can shake an entire galaxy with its force.

After the explosion, all that is left of the original star is its core. If the star has evolved enough and its core is massive enough, its gravity will cause it to collapse until it becomes a black hole. If the star's core is less massive, it may collapse until it becomes a neutron star—a lump of neutrons all squashed together into a hot, dense superliquid, or "soup."

The neutron star may be stable, or it may be massive enough to keep contracting. In the second case, some astronomers speculate that the temperature of the star will rise. The neutrons will be squeezed together even more tightly, and the neutrons' quarks will begin bumping into each other. This will create new energy, matter, and antimatter.

For every particle of matter there is an antimatter "twin," the same in all respects as the original matter except that the antimatter has an opposite electrical charge. Whenever matter and antimatter meet, they destroy each other. A star can be rocked with matter-antimatter explosions that are "fueled" by the enormous numbers of tightly packed, highly energized quarks. In short, such a star may become a "quark star."

THE NEUTRINO
AND THE UNIVERSE

You may have heard the old story about the tiny mouse who saved the life of a huge and terrible lion. It is rare for something as small as a mouse to save the life of something as big as a lion. But it can happen.

For example, scientists are eagerly studying a particle known as the *neutrino.* A neutrino is an incredibly small speck of matter, a "ghost" particle that could pass through a lead wall 20 light-years thick. Yet, as small as it is, the neutrino may one day save the life of our entire universe.

Neutrinos, like electrons and quarks, are elementary particles. The Italian physicist Enrico Fermi gave neutrinos their name to distinguish them from neutrons. In Italian *neutrino* means "little neutral one." Neutrinos lack an electrical charge, are extremely small, and have little or no mass (matter).

When the universe first began, it is thought, vast swarms of neutrinos were created by the Big Bang. And today, trillions of neutrinos are still being created every second by the fusion of hydrogen atoms in the core of our sun and other stars.

How do you trap a tiny particle that has no charge and very little or no mass? To catch some of the many neutrinos that come from our sun, physicist Frederick Reines resorted to extraordinary means. A mile underneath Lead, South Dakota, is the Homestake gold mine. In this mine Reines built a neutrino detector—a large tank filled with perchloroethylene, a chemical used in dry cleaning.

Over the last seventeen years, Reines has been trapping neutrinos. But he has been shocked by his poor catch. According to all calculations, the sun should be sending out four times as many neutrinos as Reines has been able to detect.

What happened to the other neutrinos? According to Reines, these may have mutated, or changed, into other kinds of neutrinos that can slip through the "holes" of his type of net. But if the neutrinos were able to change into other kinds of neutrinos, that means they must have mass. And neutrinos with mass will shake up some old ideas concerning the future of the universe.

Ninety percent of the universe is made up of neutrinos. If a single neutrino has mass, that means the entire universe is much more massive than astronomers had believed.

For decades, astronomers have been working on a huge problem of cosmic addition. Using all sorts of telescopes, they have been peering out into space and trying to tally up the total mass of all of the matter they see. Based on the latest calculations, astronomers have found only one or two tenths the amount of matter needed to make the universe stop expanding and collapse back in on itself.

All matter has gravity, and it is gravitational attraction that —if there is enough of it—will cause the universe to start contracting again. Without enough matter, the universe will continue to expand, with all of its various parts moving farther and farther apart. The temperature of the universe will continue to drop, the last generation of suns will eventually burn out, and the universe will die.

But a neutrino with mass changes the whole picture. All the trillions and trillions of neutrinos in the universe will give it enough mass—and thus enough gravitation—to eventually start shrinking. When the explosive force from the Big Bang becomes weaker than the gravitational attraction of all its parts, the universe will start collapsing. This collapse, which will take billions of years, will end in a "Big Squeeze," a new cosmic egg, and then, possibly, another Big Bang.

The new Big Bang will create a whole new universe out of the elementary particles of our present universe. This process could go on forever, like the expanding and contracting beat of some giant heart. Some scientists call this the "Bang-Squeeze-Bang" or "Bang-Bang-Bang" theory of the universe.

CHAPTER SIX

NEW WINDOWS ON THE UNIVERSE

The new astronomy involves new ways of looking at time, space, stars and galaxies, and the atom. But without modern space-age tools such as computers, robots, rockets, radar, lasers, and other devices, no new astronomy would be possible.

An earth-based astronomer's view of the universe is blocked or blurred by pollutants, dust particles, and water vapor in the earth's atmosphere. But that's only part of the problem. Optical astronomers, with their light-sensitive telescopes, have to do most of their work at night, when the faint light from the stars isn't drowned out by the brilliant daytime light of the sun. And they can work only on clear nights, when the sky isn't overcast.

OPTICAL WINDOWS
Earth-based astronomers are working in many different ways to improve their view. For example, they are building giant new telescopes. One of the first of a new generation of optical tele-

scopes is the Multiple-Mirror Telescope (MMT), located atop Mount Hopkins near Tucson, Arizona. The MMT has six mirrors made of shiny, highly polished aluminum. A computer coordinates the mirrors to act like a single, much larger mirror. The six mirrors work together to capture the faint light from faraway stars and send it into the lens of the telescope.

One of the MMT's first tasks was to help astronomers look at a star with the clumsy name of PG1159-035. This blue-colored star is far hotter than most other stars (including massive blue giants), and it is pulsating mysteriously. Astronomers have determined that PG1159-035 is not a distant quasar, pulsar, or neutron star, but a star right in our own galaxy, the Milky Way. They are excited because they believe the star may be ready to do something spectacular, perhaps explode.

In spite of their problems, earthbound optical astronomers can still see things very far away. Yet they want to see even farther. One way is to build bigger telescopes. The world's largest telescope is a 236-inch (590-cm) reflecting, mirror-based telescope in the Caucasus Mountains in the Soviet Union. But the University of Texas is considering building a 300-inch (750-cm) telescope, and the University of California is hoping to build a gigantic 400-inch (1,000-cm) telescope.

The Texas telescope, if built, will be formed from a mosaic of mirrors. The mirrors will be thin and light, like huge, soft contact lenses. They will also be "intelligent." Each mirror will rest on a tiny computer, and all of the computers will communicate with each other to make sure all of the mirrors are aligned just right for focusing on the faint light from distant stars and galaxies.

If built, this telescope will be able to capture starlight half again as far as the largest optical telescope in the United States, the 200-inch (500-cm) Hale Telescope on top of Mount Palomar in California.

Also, the new telescope's astronomers want their view of the universe to be clean and clear—far from the pollution and

The Multiple-Mirror Telescope

glare of highways and cities. So they plan to build their telescope 14,000 feet (4,200 m) above sea level, atop Hawaii's Mauna Kea volcano, where there are also few clouds and less water vapor than at lower altitudes. The Texas astronomers are not alone. Astronomers from countries all over the world have built telescopes on Mauna Kea to study the universe.

When optical astronomers focus on the deepest regions of space, they see some very puzzling sights. Sometimes they see objects and events in the universe that seem impossible according to all known laws of physics. For example, they have found a quasarlike object known as a *blazar* that appears to be ejecting star matter faster than 40 times the speed of light.

Similarly, astronomers looking at a strange object called SS-433, right in our own galaxy, see it whirling around like a lawn sprinkler and at the same time fleeing from our galaxy at a speed many times faster than the speed of light. They reason that if SS-433 really were traveling at this speed, it would have left our galaxy millions of years ago.

And astronomers using the MMT have recently discovered a "multi-quasar"—a cluster of five quasars that look almost exactly alike.

Astronomers know that starlight plays tricks on them. In the cases above, they believe that the impossible events they see can be explained by the time- and space-warping effects of gravitation. When objects travel at nearly the speed of light, time slows down, almost to where it stops. And objects like the quasar "quintuplets" may, in fact, be a single quasar whose light is split by gravitation into five distinct images. The source of the immense gravitation may be an invisible, massive object, possibly a black hole.

Thanks to new techniques of separating the wavelengths of light, and new methods of gathering light—such as super-fast film and computer "image tubes"—there have been a number of important recent discoveries. For example, astronomers have long known that a large star, several times the size of our sun, often ends its life in a giant supernova explosion. Such a star is actually a recycling plant for many elements, including carbon, oxygen, nitrogen, and iron. Astronomers think of supernovae as "machines" that manufacture these and even heavier elements, then distribute them around a galaxy. But what causes a supernova?

Recently, astronomers found a faraway galaxy, Fornax A, which is unusual because it appears to have been formed from two other galaxies that collided. Using spectrograms of light from Fornax A, astronomers have determined that the force of the collision may have set off a machine-gun burst of supernovae all over the galaxy.

Astronomers further speculate that supernovae that have occurred in our own galaxy, the Milky Way, may have been caused by collisions with some outer elements of the galaxy, perhaps the Small and Large Magellanic Clouds. A collision doesn't smash individual stars together, but it does create a "tidal wave" of gravity that roars through the galaxy, creating new stars and sparking old ones into supernovae.

White dwarfs are old stars, stars that have no nuclear fuel left of their own. When a white dwarf is part of a binary or multiple-star system, it may "suck" off the gas from the other star or stars nearby, causing the dwarf to heat up and become more massive. Astronomers now believe that this behavior of white dwarfs may be the biggest cause of smaller star explosions called *novae.*

When a white dwarf goes nova, it sheds its surface in a shell that bursts from the star at a speed of over 600 miles (960 km) a second. Photons blast into space in the form of gamma rays and X rays. The star suddenly becomes immensely bright, like a huge flashbulb going off. Within a few days, a star in nova might increase its brightness as much as a million times.

Astronomers say that novae and supernovae may be among the chief causes for the birth of new stars. The explosions create "superbubbles" of gases, metals, and other star debris. Looking at X-ray telescope pictures of the outer edges of these bubbles, some astronomers think they see new stars forming.

THE RADIO-WAVE WINDOW

X rays and gamma rays are harmful to life. Fortunately, these types of radiation are unable to penetrate the earth's atmosphere. But there are other radiation "windows" on the earth. Looking through them, we can catch unusual glimpses of the universe.

Our most important nonlight window to the universe is the radio-wave window. Radio waves are low-energy photons whose waves are much longer than those of visible light. Yet, like light waves, they are able to reach the earth's surface. Astronomers began detecting and recording these waves in the 1930s and 1940s using primitive radio-wave receivers. Today, radio astronomy has become one of our chief ways to explore the universe.

The largest radio telescope facility in the world stands on the plains of San Augustin in New Mexico. During the late 1970s and early 1980s, twenty-seven huge white "dishes" sprouted like giant mushrooms under the desert sun. These dishes run along railroad tracks and act as the mobile antennae of a single radio telescope known as the Very Large Array (VLA). The 82-foot (24.6-m) dishes capture radio waves from a distant object, such as a neutron star, and send them to a central computer. The computer transforms the signals into millions of numbers, analyzes these numbers, and assembles a color TV picture of the star.

Radio telescopes are becoming very powerful and sensitive. Their sensitivity has recently enabled radio astronomers to discover a relatively small cloud of dust and gas far out in space. From the relatively hot temperature of the cloud and the way it is contracting, astronomers think they may have discovered a new star just before it "turns on."

A ground view of several Very Large Array Radio Telescope antennas.

Radio astronomers are making surprising discoveries. For example, they think they have discovered a giant black hole right at the center of our own galaxy, the Milky Way. What they see is an immense whirlpool swirling with hot gases and debris from nearby stars. Inside this whirlpool may be a black hole that is gobbling up our galaxy from the inside out. Or it may be acting as a giant "garbage can" for burnt-out suns and galactic litter.

OTHER NEW TELESCOPES

The two chief ways of looking at the universe are through the optical and radio-wave windows. But there are other ways. For example, infrared rays from the sun penetrate the earth's atmosphere along with radio waves and rays of visible light. We don't see these rays, but we feel them as heat. With new infrared detectors, scientists can study how these rays affect the other planets in our solar system.

Astronomers also hope someday to build a telescope so powerful it could detect "gravitons," the mysterious particles and waves that may cause gravitation. In theory at least, matter in every corner of the universe produces gravitons that bombard the earth. Gravitons should carry with them secrets from the most distant regions of time and space.

Astronomers are excited about the mysteries they might solve if gravitons can be captured and studied. But waves produced by gravitons may be far smaller than any other sort of wave. To observe or detect one, U.S. and Russian scientists are cooperating to construct a telescope so sensitive it can measure the height of a wave whose crest is one millionth the diameter of the nucleus of an atom.

CHAPTER SEVEN

THE VIEW
FROM
OUTER SPACE

Astronomers, geologists, astrophysicists, meteorologists, and planetologists are all members of the exciting new field of space science. Space science is possible now that scientific tools no longer need be earthbound. Instead, they can be blasted through the earth's atmosphere for a closer look at the solar system and the rest of the universe.

Since December 1962, when *Mariner 2* flew by the planet Venus, there has been a steady stream of unmanned spaceships conducting missions of exploration around the solar system and taking millions of pictures. These probes were the forerunners of modern space telescopes.

Telescopes have also been mounted on huge balloons. In fact, a balloon recently carried a gamma-ray telescope high above the surface of the earth. The telescope studied two galaxies emitting large quantities of radio waves and gamma rays. The results suggest that both of the galaxies have black holes, one with as much matter as 3 billion suns.

On Sunday morning, April 12, 1981, a new era of space

science began when the U.S. Space Shuttle was launched into orbit around the earth. The Shuttle is like a huge truck. It can carry 65,000 pounds (29,250 kg) of cargo—that's the weight of five elephants—into space. Once in orbit, the Shuttle's enormous cargo doors open, and a robot arm can lift out a telescope, a satellite, or a space probe and gently place it into earth orbit.

If all goes well, the Shuttle will carry devices into space for the National Aeronautics and Space Administration (NASA), the U.S. military, the European Space Agency (ESA), and for countries and organizations all around the world. These devices may include a space laboratory, a Jupiter explorer, a probe to study Halley's Comet when it swings by the sun in 1986, and possibly a mission to Venus to map the planet's surface using radar.

The Space Shuttle will also launch two big telescopes— the Gamma-Ray Observatory (GRO) and the spectacular Space Telescope, the most powerful astronomical tool ever built. Both devices are planned to go into orbit in 1985 or 1986.

Astronomers have already mounted telescopes on high-flying airplanes. One of the most active flying telescopes today is the Kuiper Airborne Observatory (KAO), a 36-inch (90-cm) optical telescope. The telescope and a combination of computers and other instruments are mounted inside a Lockheed C-141 jet airplane.

The KAO takes off from Moffett Field in California. It carries astronomers and their equipment to 41,000 feet (12,300 m) above the Pacific Ocean to make their observations and conduct their experiments.

In the 1970s and early 1980s, American and Russian astronauts lived for weeks aboard separate scientific laboratories that orbited high above the earth. These labs were equipped with telescopes and other astronomical devices.

Americans in the *Skylab* spacecraft spent much of their time studying the sun. They took thousands of pictures of the sun's ultraviolet rays and X-ray radiation.

—45

In the late 1980s and 1990s, European and Soviet space stations will carry a number of telescopes. Astronomers are also excited about a new generation of orbiting telescopes that have recently been launched. These will capture high-energy radiation—ultraviolet rays, X rays, and gamma rays—and turn them into photographic images.

The first high-energy telescope launched into outer space was an ultraviolet-ray detector that rode aboard a V-2 rocket shortly after World War II. Twenty-five years later, in the early 1970s, high-energy telescopes accompanied the British *Ariel* and *Uhuru* rockets into outer space. The telescopes took X-ray pictures of such interesting objects as neutron stars and the strange SS-433, with its spiraling jets of gas.

A new era of high-energy observatories began in 1977 with the launch of the U.S. X-ray telescope *High-Energy Astronomical Observatory #1 (HEAO-1)*. Then, in 1978, the *HEAO-2* was launched. The *HEAO-2* (also known as "Einstein") was a hundred times more powerful than any previous X-ray telescope.

In 1979 the *HEAO-3* satellite, which included a gamma-ray telescope, was launched. The gamma rays it detects come from cosmic "hurricanes" caused by exploding galaxies and supernovae.

Gamma rays are like waves on a stormy sea. Often they are irregular and come in bursts. On March 5, 1979, the biggest burst ever recorded roared through the solar system. Gamma-ray detectors all over went off, one by one, as this wave rolled by.

The Space Shuttle Columbia, lifting off from Cape Canaveral on April 12, 1981, begins its first voyage into space.

After gathering data from the *HEAO-3* and from U.S. and Soviet satellites, astronomers discovered that the source of the superburst was N49. N49 is a nebula in the Large Magellanic Cloud, a cluster of stars outside the main disk of our galaxy. The gamma rays had traveled 170,000 light-years before reaching our solar system. Yet even after so long a journey, the rays' blast was so concentrated and intense, it arrived like a loud clap of thunder.

What could have caused such a burst of energy? Astronomers think that the rays came from an explosion that lasted only two tenths of a second. Yet this explosion released more energy than the sun will release in its entire lifetime of 10 billion years.

And what produced the explosion? Astronomers are not sure. Some feel that it might have been a vast "starquake" on an incredibly dense neutron star buried somewhere deep inside N49. Another theory is that an asteroid or planet got too near a neutron star, and the star's tidal forces of gravity tore the object apart. As the object's fragments spiraled down to the star's surface, they created a huge quantity of high-energy particles. This resulted in a tidal wave of gamma rays being blasted into space, and, by chance, the earth and the solar system were in the rays' path.

The Space Telescope, launched by the Space Shuttle, will be 43 feet (12.9 m) long and use an incredibly precise 96-inch (240-cm) mirror to capture starlight. Its pictures will be beamed by radio to astronomers at the Space Science Institute at Johns Hopkins University in Baltimore, Maryland.

Top: *an artist's conception*
of the Space Telescope.
Bottom: *the primary mirror*
(center of picture)
of the Space Telescope.

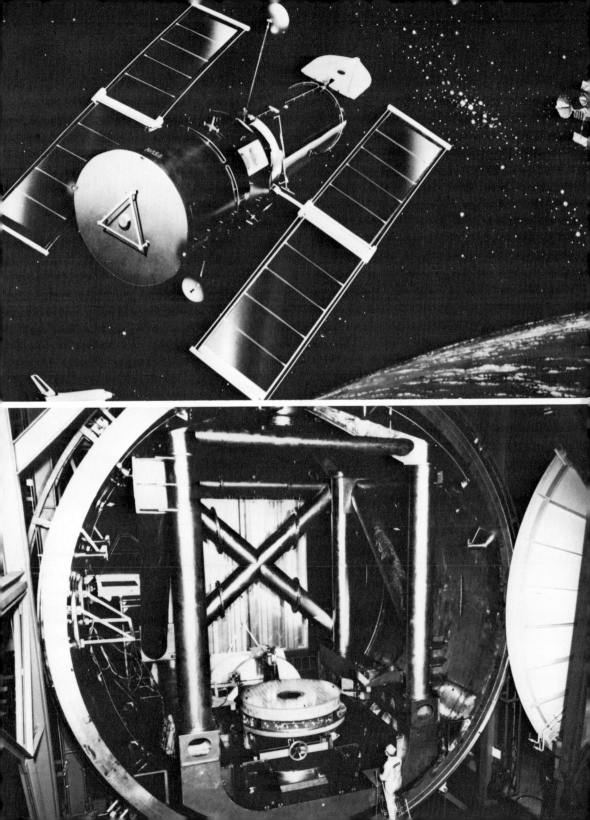

The Space Telescope isn't the first optical telescope to orbit the earth. In the early 1970s, NASA launched the small optical telescope Copernicus. And the military has a spy telescope called Big Bird that is supposedly so powerful it can read license plates in a Moscow parking lot.

But Big Bird looks only at the earth, not the universe, and Copernicus had only a fraction of the light-gathering ability the Space Telescope will have. Also, the Space Telescope will be able to study and analyze ultraviolet and infrared rays as well as visible light. Using the Space Telescope, astronomers will be able to spot objects that are 50 times fainter than those seen through earth-based telescopes. All this power will enable astronomers to look 7 times deeper into the universe.

The Space Telescope will also be pointed toward the asteroids, moons, and planets in our own solar system. It is hoped that it will be up in orbit before Halley's Comet streaks by the earth in late 1985 and early 1986. Many astronomers think that a comet is like a museum full of relics of the early days of our solar system. By studying Halley's Comet we may find clues as to how the earth was created.

The Space Telescope is exciting, but it is not the ultimate instrument of astronomy. Even more exotic telescopes are now on the drawing board. For example, there is NASA's Project Farside—a plan to build radio and optical telescopes on the far side of the moon. With the moon's low gravity, enormous telescopes could be built and maintained more easily than on the earth. They could conceivably be constructed out of materials on the moon. Looking through these telescopes, our view of the universe would be unequaled. No atmosphere would blur or distort the light or other kinds of radiation that reach the surface. And lunar rock would shield the telescopes from any noise or interference coming from the earth.

NASA scientists are also talking about building a cosmic-ray telescope in deep space. Cosmic rays are streams of sub-atomic particles that travel across space at high velocity. They are the most energetic particles we know of.

Most cosmic rays are deflected by the earth's atmosphere. (Their collision with the atmosphere produces the auroral "fireworks" we see close to the North and South Poles.) But they could be collected and measured by a cosmic-ray detector orbiting above the earth. Such a detector would be yet another tool astronomers could use to "see" objects and forces in the universe that are now almost invisible to us.

CHAPTER EIGHT

ROBOTS AND COMPUTERS

ROBOT SPACE EXPLORERS

When the United States launched its first missiles and space probes in the 1950s and early 1960s, some computers were as big as a two-story building. Military and civilian scientists wanted to put powerful computers aboard rockets, so they began a crash program to make computers smaller.

They were successful beyond their wildest dreams. A modern microcomputer is a million times more powerful than the early warehouse-sized monsters. Yet it fits within a square chip of silicon as thin as a human hair and is so tiny it could ride on the back of a ladybug.

By becoming small, computers have entered new worlds. They have turned rocket ships into robots—robots with miniature but powerful computer brains. There are robot explorers such as the *Mariner, Pioneer,* and *Voyager* spacecraft that whiz through our solar system taking pictures. There are robot orbiters, robot landers, and, soon, robot rovers that can conduct experiments and explore the surfaces of moons and planets.

The Kennedy Space Center's Hall of History in Cape Canaveral, Florida.

What business does a robot have in space?

Although it is exciting to send humans into space to take pictures and explore planets, it is cheaper and safer to send robots and remote-controlled probes. Space can be a dangerous and hostile place.

Russian cosmonauts have spent months in space in *Salyut* spacecraft—mobile homes in the sky. The Soviet Union plans to have an entire space city someday, known as Cosmograd. Yet Soviet scientists have encountered many problems trying to keep their cosmonauts healthy during long periods without gravity. The cosmonauts have had trouble keeping their food down, have been prone to infection, and have seen their muscles weaken and their bones lose calcium and turn brittle. With all these hazards and the huge expenses involved, why send humans into space to do a job robots could do as well or even better?

Robots are becoming smarter and less expensive all the time. They are far sturdier than human beings and less sensitive to the harshness of outer space. They work tirelessly twenty-four hours a day, and they take pictures and conduct experiments faster than a team of technicians working at top speed could.

A robot's eyes and ears are the telescopes, spectroscopes, and other sensing instruments aboard the spacecraft. Its brain is a computer that obeys instructions beamed up from the earth or, when radio contact with the earth is lost, obeys a program (list of instructions) stored in its memory.

The U.S. and Soviet space programs have recognized the logic of using robots, and they have sent dozens of robot explorers around the solar system. What has been learned has truly revolutionized astronomy. For example, thanks to our robots, we now know that Saturn, the Ringed Planet, has over a *thousand* rings. And joining Saturn as ringed planets are Jupiter and Uranus.

And what about Venus? Thanks to the seventeen robot explorers that have visited Venus, we now know it to be a nightmarish place, with temperatures hot enough to melt lead, bolts of lightning flashing twenty-five times a second, and a sulfuric-acid mist. The sturdy Soviet *Venera* robots that landed on Venus's surface all perished within minutes due to the planet's searing heat and crushing pressures.

Robot astronomers do more than snap pictures. They also take instrument readings and conduct numerous experiments. During the long weeks before the *Voyager* robots reached Jupiter and Saturn, they performed a steady stream of experiments and gathered billions of bits of information. On the surface of Mars, the two *Viking* landers conducted dozens of experiments, including testing for life.

Robot and remote-controlled spacecraft have also tested for the gravitational warping of space and time predicted by Albert Einstein. Astronomers think that space and time in distant parts of the universe can be altered by violent events involving very massive objects. For example, imagine that in a distant galaxy, two black holes collide. The collision of these two black holes would create a gravity "tidal wave" that would spread through the universe. Such a wave would warp and distort time and space around everything it passed. Eventually this wave might reach the earth.

If such an event occurs, scientists hope to be ready. Using a special earth-based clock, they will notice a small but definite alteration in the clock's precise timekeeping as the wave passes over the earth.

Using the information gathered from this and a similar clock that is planned to be placed in orbit around Jupiter, scientists hope to confirm the existence of so-called *gravity waves* and measure their strength. Eventually, the scientists hope to build a "gravity telescope" using a string of such clocks orbiting planets all around the solar system. The scientists think that when they "look" into the telescope, they may see things in the universe even stranger than black holes and quasars.

In the future, scientists hope to build robot explorers that

—55

journey beyond the solar system to other stars and, perhaps, to any planets orbiting these stars. Robot explorers of the future will have to be independent and intelligent in order to survive the long years of traveling.

Along the way, while waiting for new instructions from humans back on earth, the robot explorer would keep busy. It would be a multipurpose robot that would take pictures, conduct experiments, and send a constant stream of information back to the earth.

Today's robot explorers have only limited intelligence. Everything their sensors pick up is sent back to the earth. As a result, scientists are flooded with trillions of bits of information, much of it repetitive or useless. The star-hopping robot of the future will probably be much more picky. It will carefully examine everything it sees and relay only what it decides is worth mentioning to its human bosses.

A robot explorer might have several "assistants" that would travel with it to distant stars. The lead robot would orbit any planet it discovers. It would send one of the assistants to land on the planet's surface (if possible). Another assistant, maybe a robot rover, might wander around the planet performing experiments and sending pictures back to the lead robot orbiting high overhead.

Finally, the explorer robot of the future might be self-replicating. This means that it would be capable of producing offspring—other new robots. Whenever the robot found an asteroid, a moon, or a planet with enough raw materials, it would land, set up a tiny portable factory, and manufacture new robots. Some robots might be left behind to "colonize" and explore the planet and make more new robots.

COMPUTERS AND ASTRONOMY

Computers, large and small, are essential tools in the new astronomy. They are being used to produce and enhance images from telescopes and from explorer-robots' cameras.

Artists use them to convert millions of numbers into stunning pictures of planets, stars, and galaxies. Astronomers study the evolution of a star's imagined solar system or galaxy using computer "movies"—animated models displayed in color on the computer's picture screen.

Optical telescopes are often on mountaintops. Optical astronomers do their work at night. At night on the top of a mountain, it can get quite cold. There is a big door in the top of an observatory that opens at night so the telescope can peek through. Once that door is open, the observatory becomes as cold as the outside. This helps to eliminate the turbulence in the air surrounding the telescope.

Astronomers used to have to spend their nights dressed like Eskimos. They sat high atop the telescope in a cagelike structure, aiming the instrument at distant stars and taking pictures. They wore gloves with the fingertips cut off so they could handle the telescope's delicate controls. By morning, their fingertips would be bluish and numb.

But not any more. Many of the newer telescopes are computer-controlled. Astronomers report to work early in the evening. They give the night assistant the coordinates of the section of sky they want to study, the types of tests they want done, and the pictures they want taken. The assistant enters these instructions into the telescope computer's memory. The astronomer can then leave. The computer does the rest.

Astronomers are plagued by the tendency of the atmosphere to scatter and reflect light and other kinds of radiation. But there is another problem, too. When photons of light are captured by a telescope and focused on a photographic plate for a picture, most of them turn into heat or bounce off the plate without leaving an image. Out of every thousand photons that arrive from a star, only five to thirty help form the star's picture. All the rest are lost.

Astronomers are trying to increase the quality of their photographs by using new high-speed films. But the most promising technique is to replace the film with a computerized camera. A tiny computer chip covered with many light-sensing cells can trap up to eight hundred photons out of every thousand.

A computer camera converts what it "sees" into numbers. Then astronomers can use other computers to analyze these numbers and modify the pictures in a variety of ways. The computer can even create "false" colors that emphasize certain features in the picture.

For example, the astronomer can ask the computer to call up from its memory a TV picture of Jupiter's Great Red Spot, a massive storm in Jupiter's atmosphere. Then the astronomer can order the computer to highlight the colors red and blue in the picture and tone down the color green. The changes the astronomer requested would show in vivid detail the swirling gases, clouds, and chemicals of what may be the solar system's biggest storm.

Computers are useful because they can take raw numbers and electronic pulses produced from all types of telescopes— radio, ultraviolet, X ray, gamma ray, and so on—and convert them into pictures that reveal new details. The computer picture screen becomes a new window on the universe.

Parts of the universe that may be too far away for us to ever visit can be depicted by computers, too. For example, scientists at Princeton University fed into their computer millions of bits of information about the Milky Way and other galaxies with spiral arms. The computer took several hours to process all the information. Then it flashed onto a TV screen an image of what the Milky Way would look like to someone in the

*An astronomer rides
the elevating chair
to reach the "cage"
of the Hale Telescope.*

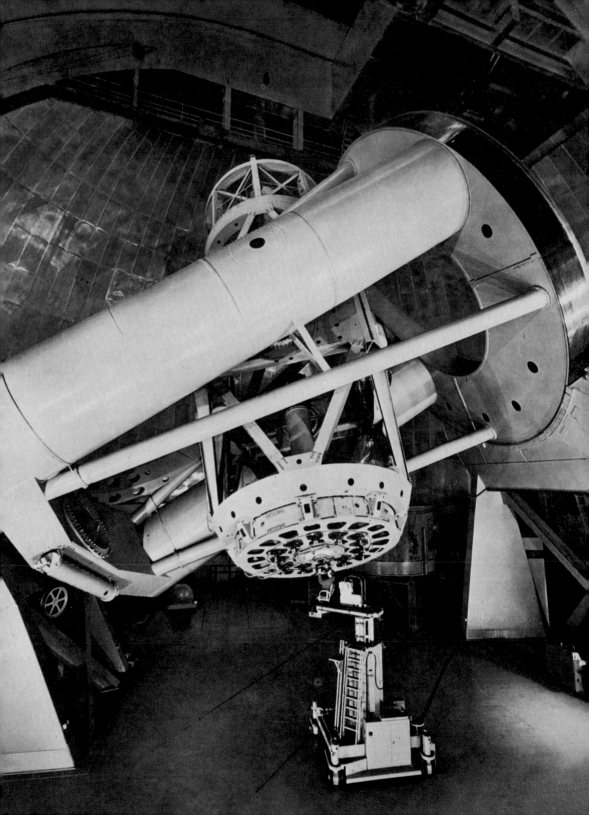

Andromeda Galaxy or in one of the Magellanic Clouds. In other words, it was a picture of our galaxy from the outside—a region of space no human or robot will visit for a long, long time.

Scientists at the Jet Propulsion Laboratory in Pasadena, California, do this sort of thing all the time. They feed their computer information from many different sources. The computer processes all of the information. Then it adds imaginary lights and shadows and comes up with an animated color "movie"—of molecules and atoms, perhaps, or a dazzling ride past Uranus and Neptune, following the scheduled path of the *Voyager 2* spacecraft in the late 1980s. Additional movies trace the evolution of the universe or witness the birth of a galaxy.

These "movies" are exciting to watch, but they are not for entertainment only. They are based on the latest available scientific data. Studying them, astronomers can see relationships between complex processes occurring in the universe.

When astronomers look through a telescope, whether the instrument is on earth or in space, much of what they see is relatively still and unchanging. This is because most events in the universe take place over thousands, millions, or even billions of years.

When we look at the universe, it is a lot like shooting a slow-motion movie of New York City from a helicopter above. Down below us the city appears to be a jumble of sights, sounds, and action. People are coming and going; cars are honking. But in our movie, when we play it back, everything is slowed down a million times. What does New York City look like then? It looks frozen. And that is the way we see much of the universe.

To see New York City in motion, we would have to speed up the action a million times. To see the universe in motion, we would have to do the same thing. This is what great astronomers and other space scientists have always done. They could see in their imagination the birth and death of stars and galaxies. From these insights, they devised their theories. The theories describe the universe in motion. The scientists rarely saw the events their theories described, but they could imagine them.

Today, astronomers and other space scientists can reproduce these events in the form of computer simulations, or models. An astronomer can refine a theory by feeding it into a computer and turning it into a computer "movie." As in a movie, events can be speeded up or slowed down. Events that would normally take place over millions of years can whiz by in a few seconds. Events that occur in a trillionth of a second can be made to last several minutes. The astronomer can run the movie forward or backward, or freeze the action and look at one "frame" at a time.

Computers also help astronomers turn rough ideas into clear, logical explanations of how the universe works. For example, scientists at the Carnegie Institution in the state of Washington built a computer model of our solar system based on the theory of planetesimals. A planetesimal is a rock or clod of dirt that moves in orbit in space. Some scientists believe that the planets of our solar system were built up from countless tiny planetesimals created during the formation of our solar system. So they built a model—a computer movie. Then they ran the movie.

In the movie, a million years were compressed into a moment. Over millions of years, the planetesimals orbiting the sun collided with each other. Sometimes they broke into tiny fragments, but often they combined. Gradually they formed larger and larger planetary bodies. In the movie, after a hundred million years, only six "planets" remained, resembling Mercury, Venus, the earth, the moon, Mars, and a small planetesimal very near the sun. Interestingly, in the movie, the planet that would correspond to the earth ended up about the size of the earth and had a hot, liquid core from being bumped into so often.

CHAPTER NINE

A NEW AGE OF DISCOVERY

Today's astronomers aren't just concerned with strange and mysterious objects in remote corners of the universe. They know that astronomy can also act as a mirror to help us better understand the earth, and thus ourselves. By studying astronomy we learn to see ourselves and our tiny planet as part of the solar system, a galaxy, and the universe. We learn how objects and forces in the universe have shaped life on earth, how they continue to affect us, and how they might influence our future. And there is always more to learn.

In the mid-nineteenth century, the great scientist Michael Faraday gave a speech in which he spoke with extreme confidence. "The great laws of physics," he said, "have all been discovered. The only thing that remains is for physicists to work out the details."

Not too many years later, the twentieth century arrived, and physicists discovered that the universe was exploding. They found that black holes may really exist, and that time and space could be twisted, stretched, squeezed, and warped. It was the beginning of a whole "new physics." Dozens of new natural laws were discovered; many old laws were revised or simply discarded.

As we eagerly await the launch of the Space Telescope and the development of other new and powerful devices that will "see" into space, one thing is certain: Our current understanding of the universe is greater than ever before. Yet it is still imperfect and subject to change.

In the seventeenth century, the leaders of the Inquisition forced one of the first new astronomers, Galileo, to publicly deny that the earth orbited the sun. But Galileo was right. Maybe some of today's astronomers with unusual ideas will become, like Galileo, the creators of a new astronomy of the future.

Today's astronomy is a combination of old and new mysteries and ancient and new tools. But most of all it is a new generation of astronomers who are determined to probe even deeper than their predecessors into the secrets of space. Let's follow them on their continuing voyage of exploration and discovery!

GLOSSARY

Antimatter—the opposite of matter. For every kind of matter, there is a kind of antimatter that has an equal mass but an opposite charge. If matter and antimatter collide, they explode, releasing a huge quantity of energy.

Atom—the smallest possible unit of an element. There are over a hundred basic elements that exist in the universe, including gases such as hydrogen and oxygen and metals such as gold. An atom consists of a core, or nucleus, of neutrons and protons, and electrons orbiting around the nucleus.

Black hole—according to theory, a massive star that has collapsed and become so small and dense that it might actually rip a hole in the universe. The gravitational pull from a black hole may be so strong that not even light can escape it.

Blazar—an object that resembles a quasar because it is relatively small and generates a lot of energy. A blazar differs from a quasar in that it varies in the amount of light it radiates, has little or no X-ray emissions, has a single center or nucleus, and doesn't radiate energy along a normal spectrum.

Cosmic rays—streams of very energetic particles moving at the speed of light through space. Cosmic rays consist of atomic nuclei and elementary particles. They come from stars and, perhaps, supernovae explosions.

Doppler effect—an apparent change in the frequency of sound, light, and other waves of radiation; caused by a change in the distance between the source of the wave and the receiver.

Electromagnetic spectrum—the radiation "windows" onto the universe. These include radio waves, microwaves, infrared radiation, visible light, ultraviolet rays, X rays, gamma rays, and cosmic rays.

Electron—a negatively charged elementary particle that has very little mass. The electron orbits around the nucleus inside an atom or it exists freely in space.

Fusion—the process by which the nuclei of light atoms (such as hydrogen) combine to form a heavier atom (such as helium). Fusion releases an enormous amount of energy. It is the process responsible for the heat and light generated by the sun and other stars.

Galaxy—a large group of stars all held together by their mutual gravitation; a "star island." There are, perhaps, more than a hundred billion galaxies in the universe. Our own galaxy, the Milky Way, is spiral shaped.

Gravitation (also *gravity*)—the attraction all objects with mass have for all other objects. Gravity is responsible for keeping moons in orbit around planets and planets in orbit around the sun. Gravity pulls us "down" toward the center of the earth.

Light-year—the distance that light travels in one earth year— almost 6 trillion miles.

Nebula (pl. *nebulae*)—a large cloud of gas and dust floating in space.

Neutrino—a very small elementary particle with no detectable electrical charge and little or no mass. Produced by the fusion process going on inside the sun and other stars.

Neutron—a particle in the nucleus of an atom. Neutrons have a relatively large mass but no electrical charge.

Neutron star—when a massive star explodes in a supernova explosion, its core may collapse into a neutron star—a star that consists only of very densely packed neutrons.

Nova (pl. *novae*)—a star that explodes. After exploding, the star suddenly becomes much brighter for a time.

Photon—a particle of energy that travels at the speed of light. Photons at different energy levels take on the different forms of radiation in the electromagnetic spectrum—from low-energy radio-wave radiation to high-energy gamma rays.

Proton—a relatively large particle with a positive charge that exists inside the nuclei of all atoms. The lightest element in the universe, hydrogen, has a nucleus that consists of a single proton.

Pulsar—a quickly rotating neutron or quark star that emits frequent, high-powered bursts of radiation.

Quark—one of the fundamental building blocks of matter. Quarks make up the protons and neutrons inside an atom.

Quasar—a starlike (*QUA*si-*Stell*A*R*) object that appears to be distant and traveling at a high speed away from us. If this is true, quasars emit an unbelievable amount of energy by some unknown process.

Radar ("*RA*dio *D*etecting *A*nd *R*anging")—a device, like a radio transmitter, for finding the presence or location of an object by measuring the time it takes for the echo of a radio wave to return from the object. For example, large radio transmitters on earth can bounce radio signals off the moon and nearby planets to obtain accurate measurements of their distance.

Radiation—energy traveling at high speeds through space in the form of waves or particles; emanations from the sun.

Relativity—a group of theories concerning time, space, and motion proposed by Albert Einstein and others. One theory says that what we see is *relative* to our acceleration or how close we are to an object.

Spectrogram—a "photograph" of radiation (such as starlight) broken down into separate wavelengths. Spectrograms are often used to determine the elements present in a star and the star's temperature and motion.

Supernova—a giant star explosion; only occurs with very massive stars.

White dwarf—a star that has collapsed, perhaps as a result of a nova. One of the last possible phases of a star's life. The star's nuclear fuel has all been used up, but the star shines faintly until it completely cools down (and becomes a "black dwarf").

FOR FURTHER READING

MAGAZINES

Astronomy. (monthly) P.O. Box 92788, Milwaukee, WI 53202. $18 per year.

Griffith Observer. (monthly) Griffith Observatory, 2800 East Observatory Road, Los Angeles, CA 90027. $5 per year.

Sky and Telescope. (monthly) Sky Publishing Corporation, 49 Bay State Road, Cambridge, MA 02138. $14 per year.

BOOKS

Asimov, Isaac. *Asimov on Physics.* New York: Avon Books, 1979.

———. *Building Blocks of the Universe.* New York: Abelard, 1974.

———. *Quasar, Quasar, Burning Bright.* New York: Avon Books, 1979.

Calder, Nigel. *Einstein's Universe.* New York: The Viking Press, 1979.

———. *The Key to the Universe: A Report on the New Physics.* New York: The Viking Press, 1977.

Gallant, Roy A. *A National Geographic Picture Atlas of Our Universe.* Washington, DC: National Geographic Society, 1980.

Henbest, Nigel. *The Exploding Universe.* New York: Macmillan Publishing Company, Inc., 1979.

Kaufmann, William J., III. *Black Holes and Warped Spacetime.* San Francisco: W. H. Freeman and Company, 1979.

Lampton, Christopher. *Black Holes and Other Secrets of the Universe.* New York: Franklin Watts, 1980.

Lawton, A. T. *A Window in the Sky.* New York: Pergamon Press, 1979.

Marten, Michael, and John Chesterman. *The Radiant Universe.* New York: Macmillan Publishing Company, 1980.

Motz, Lloyd. *The Universe: Its Beginning and End.* New York: Charles Scribner's Sons, 1976.

INDEX

Gravity, 17, 21, 24-27, 35, 39, 43; waves, 55

Hale Telescope, 37
Halley's Comet, 45, 50
Herschel, William, 12
High-Energy Astronomical Observatory (HEAO): *#1*, 46; *#2*, 46; *#3*, 46, 48
Hubble, Edwin, 10, 12-14, 15

Infrared rays, 23, 43, 50

Jupiter, 45, 54, 55, 58

Kepler, Johannes, 10
Kuiper Airborne Observatory (KAO), 45

Laplace, Pierre, 16
Lasers, 36
Lemaître, Georges, 14
Leptoquarks, 31
Light waves, 21, 23, 39, 41, 57; shift of, 13-14

Mariner spacecraft, 44, 52
Mars, 55, 61
Matter, 27, 28-35
Mercury, 61
Meteors, 10
Microwaves, 15-16, 23
Milky Way, 12, 37, 40, 43, 58, 60
Molecules, 28, 30
Moons, 50
Movies, computer, 61
Multiple-Mirror Telescope (MMT), 37, 39

National Aeronautics and Space Administration (NASA), 45, 50
Nebulae, 13-14, 27, 48
Neptune, 60
Neutrinos, 8, 29, 30, 33-35
Neutron stars, 23, 25, 31, 33, 46, 48
Neutrons, 30
N49, 48
Novae, 40-41

Optical telescopes, 8, 17, 36-39, 43, 45, 48, 50, 57

Particle accelerators, 29
Peebles, P. J. E., 15-16
Penzias, Arno, 15-16
PG1159-035 (star), 37
Photons, 23, 40, 41, 57
Pioneer spacecraft, 52
Planetesimals, 61
Planets, 28, 43, 48, 50, 61. *See also* names of planets
Pollution, 36, 37
Positrons, 31
Project Farside, 50
Protons, 29; death of, 29-31
Pulsars, 31

Quark stars, 31-33
Quarks, 8, 29, 30-31
Quasars, 27, 39, 55

Radar, 36
Radiation, 17, 21, 23, 29, 40-43, 46. *See also* types of radiation
Radio telescopes, 41, 43
Radio waves, 15-16, 23, 31, 41-43, 44, 58
Reines, Frederick, 34
Robot space probes, 8, 36, 52-56
Rockets, 36

Salyut spacecraft, 54
Saturn, 54, 55
Schmidt, Maarten, 27
Shift, 13-14
Singularity, caused by a black hole, 24-25
Skylab, 45
Slipher, Vesto, 13-14, 15
Sound waves, 13
Soviet Union, 37, 43, 45, 46, 48, 54, 55
Space probes, robot, 8, 36, 52-56
Space Shuttle, 45, 48
Space Telescope, 8, 45, 48, 50, 63
Spectrograms, 12, 40
Spectrograph, 12
SS-433, 46